THE NECESSITY OF SYMBOLS

THE NECESSITY OF SYMBOLS

Thomas Ramey Watson

 **Barn Swallow Media**

THE NECESSITY OF SYMBOLS

Barn Swallow Media
Denver, CO

Copyright © 2013 Thomas Ramey Watson
ISBN: 0-9818430-2-6
ISBN-13: 978-0-9818430-2-5
LCCN: 2013919991

LIBRARY OF CONGRESS CATALOGING-IN-PUBLICATION
DATA
The Necessity of Symbols / Thomas Ramey Watson. p.cm.
ISBN-13: 978-0-9818430-2-5 (alk. paper)
1. Poetry. 2. Spirituality. 3. Signs. 4. Symbols.
5. Incarnational Theology. 6. Sexuality. I. Title.

Cover design by Cheryl Ramirez
www.CCRBookCoverDesign.com
Cover art is of a painting by Ivo, which I own.

Contents

Foreword: What Body?

You still believe the body is a temple for the spirit? Then read Thomas Ramey Watson and be delighted and appalled with him! *The Necessity of Symbols* plays again and again on the sacredness of the body—the body in love, the body in ecstasy of spirit and memory, even the body of Christ in communion.

Like the forgotten troubadours, the poet gives a credible poetic ground that loving the beloved's body is close to loving God, or at least appreciating the universe. "Knot Intrinsicate" celebrates a woman's power:

I am seventeen—
you, soft-voiced Guenevere.
But a Russian doll,
you held inside Mary,
hawk of Catholicism,
and Cleopatra,
salad of the crescent world:
eaten—undone—whole again.

In a long poem that summarizes loss of job, loss of wife, loss of environment (Colorado), the poet holds psalms and songs in memory step by step of the way, shoring up the many threats to his spiritual life ("A Book of Hours"):

My mind
stayed on echoes:
whether one eats

9

God's words,
or wakes
within them—
does upheaval
always follow?

In the poem, "Holy Communion," the poet does not scruple to equate the host with two lovers, who, as the poem progresses are separated, however, with the finite limits between them implicitly contrasted to God's infinite love: "Broken from you, / I am set on a shelf." However, the lover remains an inspiration:

Rising
past the fragrance of ankles and thighs,
lingering on chest and neck, to pause
on tiny moles like cinnamon
sprinkled about your mouth

that explored with words, and tongue,
and smile, then to those eyes,
brown as buttered crust on fresh-baked bread;
still I hear your voice, yeasty, low.

These are fine points of a book with a broad sweep— poems about family, poems contrasting the poet's native Denver with the signal cultural meccas of Europe, poems most often of joy. The range is admirable and the poems intricate and dedicated to spiritual growth, with creation the touchstone where reality is tested and embodied.

Alan Naslund, author of *Silk Weather*

Meditation

I stood with you
under the arches
of the Denver Center,
the damp stones rising
in various angles.
The changing light,
the grey subtleties
reminded me of Tours,
so different from the steady topaz
that lights Assisi's pink
and golden stones,
flaky as crusts
on fresh-baked bread.

Touching my mouth
with one finger—three—
then your mouth—
you embraced me,
the warmth of your body
pressed against mine.

I sit
on a low brick wall,
watching
as you walk away,
a miniature
in my book of hours.

Mykonos Turn

My hands about your waist,
we motorcycle from familiar terrain—
cell-like rooms at Maria's,
stony beach where one man
wears no clothes,
village where men
and women mince
over designer fashions
and five windmills sign
a past no longer useful—

beyond—

pigeons fly
from square, whitewashed
beehive-roosts;
donkeys roam
among chickens—
sunflowers.

Pavement—
gravel.

I lean into you—
geraniums on the ridge—
dolphins—
shingles sing.

At Nafplion

Potsherd-beach—
blaze of sun on winter flesh—
wind blowing through hair
fresh-washed like clothes
on makeshift lines.

That is not all: love
is the curve of body
on body,
your head
on my chest like a buoy.

Incarnation

Note-sized flakes of snow fell
while we stood at my window
and examined the small, scalloped hole
made in the glass by a boy bullied
from the schoolyard across the street.
"I saw him falter, turn inward: the pebble
passed through the aspens and hit my window,"
I explained, tracing the lines
which crossed where the stone struck,
the vertical axis longer than the horizontal.
"A star has signed the glass."

I showed you two long-bearded kings—
their bodies like grasshoppers—engraved
on the upper corners of the brass frame
of my fireplace, "see, just inside the green
ceramic leaf-tiles—1890 originals."
Smiling, you said, "No, those figures
are magicians." Placing your wine glass
on the white wood mantle, you bent
to examine the fire-lit emblems with both hands.
Perhaps they're magi, we decided,
envisioning artisans who built Denver
and signed it with themselves.

Coinherence

Cold blue lakewater laps
against granite rocks beneath us,
making sounds like sucking mouths.
Juice from Grand Junction watermelon
rivulets down our chins and forearms.

Last night you traced my life
in your wine-stained palm.
Holding you, I dreamed a hologram
of galaxies waxing in your menses.

Music of the Spheres

Last night—my hands holding
pendant worlds—I listened
to the hieroglyphs
of synchronized breath.
Crowned by the solar disk,
the hawk held the uraeus.

This morning we sit on the cabin balcony,
sipping a strong, French blend.
In the piney distance
a dog barks, a lark sings—
then the neighbor's telephone.

Sounds ring like pebbles
on silent surfaces.
Like your mouth, Sunshine Canyon opens
to christen car- and house-dusted
plains below.

A Colorado Spring

We sat and drank red wine from paper cups.
Tracing our lives, laughing,
across open palms, we shared
the six apricot roses I'd brought.

We no longer share
red wine in paper cups, or apricot roses.
The damp of April washes green
into greys, frozen.

Now I meet other faces, eyes and arms,
and mouths.
            But rising from a flat horizon
the curve of the instep still leads
upwards to you.
You took my hands—
my palms are stained cerise,
my fingers—the petals of a rose.

Knot Intrinsicate

Grapefruit-halves like a split
and hollowed sun—
croissants, marmalade;
porcelain coffee pot, window table:
the Old Poodle Dog
on leaf-strewn Sloane Square.

Oboe-voiced, you break silence,
suggest help
with connections.
I call back laughter,
deepening faces:
women who walked always
along the sea's green edge.
Waves whip—
shawls about the shoulders.

I am seventeen—
you, soft-voiced Guenevere.
But a Russian doll,
you held inside Mary,
hawk of Catholicism,
and Cleopatra,
salad of the crescent world:
eaten—undone—whole again.

Strong toil of grace.

Outside
last night's snow shook

from Denver aspens
like bread crusts on coffee-stained soil.
White room of winter—
telephone near—
I circle
silent as a bell.

Redaction

I spoke love—she held me
within the boundaries of her skirts,
but I could not play—
could not relinquish
intellect for anyone.
Rutted like a phonograph record
overplayed, I stopped spinning—
no longer turning on command.

Her crying fits, attempted suicide—
knife thrust at my hand with pleas
to cut her from the misery—
her threats of leaving—
no longer on my knees:
                   no preparation,
no opiate can blunt
the knife's edge at the bone.

The Necessity of Symbols

But now, to the best of our ability we use symbols
appropriate to things Divine, and from these
again we elevate ourselves, according to our degree,
to the simple and unified truth of the spiritual vision.
Pseudo-Dionysius, *On Divine Names*

All morning the rain fell, sounding
on the roof like round, grey pebbles.
At noon the sky cleared to a translucent lapis.
On the chaise lounge over red bricks
I lay sunbathing, the air steamy,
the sun a bright, gold alpha.

I thought of my students' exercises in poetry.
One told of his grandmother's taking him,
a chubby-handed toddler, to Washington Park.
There she showed him ducks, told him
he walked as well as they, taught him to count—
one duck, two ducks, three—
white, and brown, and mottled.

In Washington Park one green day in April
I watched the meridian sun fall
and take residence in your hair;
my vision followed the curve of descent
as you bent to feed the ducks
crusts from your sandwich.

We felt like children ourselves.
Together we relearned our numbers,
how Dionysius stooped on Aegean sands
to demonstrate that one becomes two—then three—
enlarging
until by love all returns to one again.

My front side as cerise as the nearby peonies,
I turned and lay on my stomach.
A bead of sweat gathered on my temple, broke,
and ran into my eye.
Stinging light—refracting—the bead multiplied.
Three drops fell in opaque pools that dried
quickly on the heme-baked bricks below.

Augustinian Paradoxes

In Lincoln, Nebraska, you keep your vigil.
Near Vail, Colorado, I sit at the window
watching bats returning to their caves
against the reddening sky.
I recall your voice,
how the pitch turned and fell
when you told me your father
had suffered a massive stroke.
An alcoholic you've come to love
suffers his dimming.

Even in eclipses may we seek
the pure undivided black light
that some say is God's, found
through following the steep turnings
along sheer cliffs that lead to Him,
even as that blood-dark light leads,
sounding me, to you.

A Book of Hours

1

Four a.m., February 14:
I wake to a four-part hymn—
an invisible choir—
words of a river,
and God.

Words like lasers—
in double columns—
as in Bibles—
blaze from my walls
and ceiling.

I bristle to attention—
but cannot read—
Greek? Hebrew?
Or English?
All out of focus
for myopic eyes.

Desiring to get my glasses—

I fear the music
and words
will fade.

2

My wife—snoring
in her own bedroom—

flashes
into my mind.

Like Baucis,
she rises
to set out milk
and cereal
for a heavenly visitation.

But when Ezekiel and John
ate God's words,
the syllables
like halvah in their mouths
proved ipecac.

3
April 12:
the college where I teach
shuts my department
like a book.

I step up my search
for the hymn
I've heard.

4
A Baptist hymnal:
humming, I recognize
the words and tune—
by Havergal—
"Like a river glorious
is God's perfect peace,

over all victorious
in its bright increase . . ."

5
May 25:
wife moves out—
taking one cat.
Leaves me
with the other,
lawn chairs,
and a bed.
Files for divorce.

6
Months of wandering.

I flee to Kentucky—
to finish graduate school.
Like a book,
Colorado—
home for three generations—
seems closed
forever.

7
Worn like a hair shirt—
through time
and place:
Havergal's chorus,
"Stayed upon Jehovah,
hearts are fully blessed,
finding, as He promised,
perfect peace and rest."

8

A decade later—
still moving
toward the sun:
I walk the Cam
and stones
to Ridley.

My mind
stayed on echoes:
whether one eats
God's words,
or wakes
within them—
does upheaval
always follow?

Crossroads

In the blue-white light
of the deserted Denver street five cats
silently scatter to crouch in the shadows
of nearby lawns and stare as I approach.
Overhead, the scoldings of a lone grackle

flitting from tree to tree
disturbs the June pool-surface silence.
On the pavement a wounded male grackle,
unable to fly, hobbles, inches at a time,
falls, goes on, falls again,

pausing as he nears, to see
how much I threaten.
His companion—louder—diving,
allows me to see
a streak of green iridescence

on her black sides.
Some madness persuades her that her mate
might get to safety,
fly again.
And I?

How badly is the grackle wounded?
He will not let me near.
Should I find a stone and knock him in the head—
as I just did to the abscessed cat
hit by a car beside the Via Appia?

But I do nothing,
let nature take her course—
the terrified squallings of the cat
amid ruined Roman statuary
flooding all memory.

I return home: glad of bricks
I'm careful to lock the door,
hoping that some of the world's barbarians
do not wound me—

or, if so, that they are quick,
that I will not have to lie
waiting for some compassionate hand,
or be forced to hobble on,
hoping to outrun them, without
even a mate to cry.

Hieroglyphs

A circus tent near Cherry Creek—
buying plants for my new house.
Sudden thunder—hail heaping
like grain—whirlpooling rain.
Your body, warm
like fresh-baked bread,
against my chest.
Confession from a doctor
whose mother
trained her not to cry—
whispers, shaking.

Skies cleared to blue milk;
you paid the clerk.
We carried two miniature crepe myrtles
to your car.
I told you how I felt to stand
before the Rosetta Stone
for the first time:
black basalt tablet—
key to the riddles
of reedy instruments
and incense,
where lovesick Isis,
like the Nile, rose to gather
her rice-strewn lover.

Couscous in November:
my middle finger smashed—
chrysanthemum petals

on the table—
Telephone call in May:
you're marrying—
will I come?

He believes in institutions.
Do I think it will be all right?

"Yes,

I too believe in the Pentagon,"
I reply.
Childlike:
"you are my standard."
"Poodle?" I wonder.

Phone on the table.
Image of you
before a full-length mirror:
wedding gown and veil.

Glasses off,
I put on medieval music—
shawms, wooden flutes,
sackbuts, krummhorns.

Flu

Down two blocks the bells of St. Catherine's
sound in a grey string, two-toned, long.
Someone has died.
Room dark, I lie on my bed.
The rain floods in crooked fingers
down the window pane.

Mercurial
I'm slipping
down to the bottom of the bed,
over the edge—in a grey wash
that falls down yet another pallet,
darker, hands failing—over that
to another edge.

We talk on a black telephone.
I'm reaching—wrestling
with memory.
What did the sun in a green glinting
that apotheosized us
sound like?
My mind, a closed fist,
is a knot of bells.

Outside, the irises are unfolding,
one petal at a time,
shawl-like fingers
that flamenco around arcane mouths.
The indigo iris has opened.

Its petals, deep, heavy with rain, fall
downward through green swords
in syllables of purple.

Family Portraits

A rosebush
grows from her face,
and from his,
a beefsteak tomato
that bears profusely—
gravemarkings offered
with open hands
by grown children.

Petal-like
Grandmother felt her family
inferior to Grandfather's
with hardy torsos,
long limbs, fleshy faces.
This green man
dusted by Great Plains
was buried in his Stetson.

In memory's eye
I scan familiar faces—
aunts, uncles, mother, father,
sibs, exes—my own.
I recognize the arabesques
that threaten entire lines.

Perhaps marking our headstones
with etchings of the unconscious,
drawing them to waking,
reciting them with grave inscriptions

about love potions, poisoned fruit
will release us from their power—
fairy tale,
joke grown profound.

Companion Portraits

She holds and rocks me, a child
of two—five—then seven,
singing in a reedy voice
of brave soldier boys,
who never trembled,
even facing rockets' flares,
and bruised slave boys
comforted on mamas' laps.

I see her with lilacs, with violets
that grow in her yard,
their leaves heart-shaped and flowers
heavy with scent and purple—
and golden wheat, the color of her hair
and flesh, and plains of Northeastern Colorado,
where Grandmother, Grandfather and I
drive on summer days, drinking water
from a mason jar—zinc-tasting, sun-heated wine—
through what seem days as endless
and clear and rolling as Western skies.

But on another page, I see her great,
knotted, farmwife hands
always reaching, stretching, petting
children, grandchildren, then great-grandchildren—
searching for the right door—
knob after knob after knob—
in an endless hall of mirrors—
where, like the ocean, the prince
sweeps in, removing his blue beard,

and rocks away—smoothes away
generation
after generation of sorrow.

Correspondence

1

Two letters arrive in the mail
from great-aunts who live
where the South Platte bends
like an old woman
in northeastern Colorado.

Ruth is offended that I surmised grief
at her husband's passing:
slobbering, spoon-fed, diapered,
wearing a body that he could not control,
Fred had spent three years in a nursing home.
She feels no grief:
they had a perfect marriage,
happiness that's rare.
Three pages full.

I thought it natural to grieve,
even if one loved well.
But I've never had a marriage
from the happy fairy tale.

Ethel, my other aunt, advises
that I must be content to be alone,
now that I've been divorced and failed,
throw my energies into church, work,
students, and yard.
She loves me (Ruth reminds me
that she does too)—
and doesn't want to see me crumpled again.

Seeing so much misery roll like storm
after storm over the prairie,
Ethel never wanted to date:
as the eldest sister
life offered her no slipper.

Ethel was always serious, too serious,
I hear my grandmother, her sister, say.

And Ruth, the youngest,
who fashioned herself a Cinderella,
was spoiled, always got her way—
even a husband who said
her shoes were like thimbles,
her dresses made of birds' wings—
and her voice—

Why, we wondered, my sisters and I.
We heard only a Victrola
playing the same three tunes.
Fred made good money (though our grandparents
made more), weren't their children tops
(even though their daughter spun only for Fred),
wasn't life grand (despite Fred's
being gassed in France in the War).
Like a good dog, Fred took his bone,
never objected, never complained.

Dear Ethel, I'd like to write,
does pretense, like ether,
put the heart to sleep?
When you felt like a letter

fading into invisible ink,
and I—as my mother before me—
was sent like an envelope
to stay with you,
you kept the curtains shut,
afraid the dark man you dreamed
spied at your window
would gain entrance,
find, and tear—
You said he was the devil,
and hid, hoping he wouldn't see.
But he spotted you,
crouching in a corner, under a table—
came crashing—
to write like a real-life author
on the heart's delicate parchment.

I thought the man was death,
who took your two young brothers
before you could plant them
like two strong saplings
in your own walled garden
where poverty and unhappiness
would never gnaw again.
Or was the man the lover you never had?
Instead, you dreamed
and found surrogate comfort
in a young, safe, niece's—
then nephew's—hand.

2

My mother writes
that the year Aunt Ethel told her,
"Well, I guess you won't marry at this late date
but will be like me for life,"
was the year Mother met
and married my father.

Proving that she was still
of marriageable quality at twenty-seven,
she traded college and a career in art
for violence
that lasted fifteen years and three children.

Something to Do with Our Hands

Dirt drops to the ground
in little balls like pie crust dough.
Anemones planted beside the door,
we drive to the nursing home in town.

Thin as a stalk of wheat,
Aunt Ethel slides beneath her restraints
and shuffles our way.
"At ninety three"—we scold—
"you'll fall again and never go home."
She nods, "I know, I know,"
her eyes like marbles rolling in a jar.

Through corridors of bodies
like cracked or empty vases,
I wheel her,
wondering if she'll bolt.

Mother holds the door:
square by square of sidewalk.
Gibbous patio.
Impelled by inner weather,
I envision a sea of tulips
circling the grounds.

"Ethel wants your hand," Mother nudges.
"I've had a good day—" Ethel mutters,
"we'll call it square—
see how strong my arms are."
Inside, I kiss her cheek.

We tie her in her chair and walk away.
I turn. Hands on the wheels,
Ethel rocks,
as if ready for a race.

Whoosh of the outer door.
Rolling lawns. Square garden.
Rose canes begin to green.

Jacob's Ladder

Suggesting that I get the shotgun
to shoot down Grandmother's ideals,
Grandfather told me how his father
demonstrated that women were fools—
why, if he dangled his foot out the window
for ten minutes, he'd have a woman
like a ring circling every toe.

Grandfather's cynicism reflected in his limp,
his hip displaced in a branding accident
years before—fitting, he said,
for this world of spawning-ditch and boneyard.
I'd seen him cry twice, first at my wedding—
he'd caught a cold, he said—
nothing about the course of married love
could make him tearful—
and again at my grandmother's funeral:
guarding himself like a watchdog,
he muttered, "Poor Mom,
someday we'll be together again."

No one expected Grandmother
to leave first:
like the wheat,
she would show fresh,
green shoots each fall.
Every winter Grandfather said that
he wouldn't see the violets that
would in spring put up their heads.
Her nerves reacting,

Grandmother increased her pace,
her hands ever-flying.

After her death from cancer
that rooted in the thigh,
I dreamed a rolling field
where Grandmother—her hair waves of gold again,
her eyes shining as Colorado sky—
sat, laughing quietly.
"I guess I'll have to learn
to get things right," she said,
her hands at last sparrows
that had come to roost,
her warmth the fragrance
of fresh-baked bread.

Psalm

As the South Platte threads down
from its source near Alma,
I follow an eastern route.
Grasp—like flailing umbilicals—
Missouri, Mississippi,
then Ohio.

I scan,
photograph albums,
music, books, art objects.
But men, wives and children
clutch dogs
and speak a Bedouin
vaguely familiar.

This is the green valley.
This, the dark—the twenty-third.
Three sisters sit
over broken pots
babbling like wheels.
Whirl. Whirling. Whirlwind.
Voice—
Josephs' coats—
cut threads.

Conversion

Shuffled like Tarot cards
these poems tell
how the hanged man drops,
drops,
then—like mercury—
rides up his pulley—
rising above pines—
then—diving like a hawk—
uses his rope
as a bridle
on the executioner's horse.

With his rider the horse
canters into a rose garden
watered by four streams
from four cardinal directions.
Hanging midair,
Death's scythe
circles
like a falcon—
like a pocket watch
palmed by the night sky.

Grave Notions

I once imagined Lazarus
lying in his bed
   about to die
saying with some eloquence,
"Do not despair
   at my visage,
at the skulled hollow
of my cheek, or
   at the sorrow
in my darkened eye:
when the sight and hearing go,
the other senses
   soon will follow,
but the heart
   by the devouring mouth
will grow."
   Testimony of suffering
and heart's transcendence given,
     he died,
everyone impressed and edified.

I no longer think that.
No doubt Lazarus
   held out to the last,
hoping Jesus would come,
heal him of pain
   that raged instead of eloquence
in brain and tongue.
His friends and family
    were, I suppose,

even more anxious.
Jesus had been sent for—
                    hadn't come—
he could heal him,
                if he would.
Where was this master
they believed in?

When he did arrive,
                    it was
too late. Lazarus was dead.
The stink of decay
                was upon him.
His death had been
                    no act of transcendence
but one of dismay, grief,
                        disappointment.
God once more had failed.
Jesus had given hope—
                    God visible in human affairs—
but he was limited,
                took his time.
Miracle here and there,
but suffering was still
                    the order of the day.
Jesus, oblivious to the fact,
                        and to the stench—
or did he hold ins nose
                    while he wept—
called dead Lazarus
                back.

Even then,
        I doubt if Lazarus
was eloquent.
Surely he still smelled,
                knew he had died once
and left this sorrow.
Now he to do that
            again.
Or, did Jesus
        in raising him
erase the smell
        of death
        and memory?

I would rather
        have stayed dead,
        my soul in heaven.

Iconoclasm

Bernini and his friends
               appeal to me:
beautiful souls,
               beautiful experiences,
in beautiful bodies—
               reality equaling appearance,
God's beauty apprehended.

St. Teresa, ecstasy
               in the angle of her head
and lovely limbs exposed,
               with an angel of Jesus standing by,
ministering his darts of love
               thrust into her with sweet
pain, lovely dyings.

Then I discover how homely
               St. Teresa really was—
pug-faced, short and fat—
               despite her visions—
and I am left
        Jesus,
               with a hammer for my notions.

St. Joan

Thighs, naked, slashed, seared
by the flames' hungry tongues—
heaving breast, shrill
cry, hair cracked in light
about your blackening face—

I tried to tell them—
not guilty—but the church,
an often man-tongued beast
crossed once
and one might die.

Your words—words—in my ears,
the sackcloth robes against
my thighs, I waded
into the river. In the reeds
I knelt. So I knelt

before your pyre.
Now I ask if fire and water,
earth and air, ever
still the phoenix, or the turtle.
Truth and beauty may

be buried for a time,
but in cinders
the reedy song rustles—
new wings are always
                making.

Easter Morning

The bells of St. Elizabeth's ring out the hour:
the high voices, dedicated to certain saints,
ring first; the low, to sturdy others,
take up the call and bid us rise
and come away, away.

The rooster crowing in the friary yard
reminds us that we've strayed.
Here loveliness, like poppies, fades
and passes quite away.

Come, the bells of St. Elizabeth's say.
Eternity signals in every hour,
bids us climb, and ring
this bright and one, eternal day.

Palacio Real, Madrid

Our guide cautions us not to think the Flemish
tapestries faded. They are the finest in all
the royal apartments, she says. Much gold in the cloth
mutes their colors and makes each tapestry
weigh over sixty kilograms. You must allow
yourselves time to adjust and note especially
the fine details, the expressions,
the wrinkles on the faces.

That is just it. Out of this aureate,
though multi-hued, haze arise faces,
a crowd of faces, intently, devoutly gathered
about Mary, about Christ and his apostles.
All else recedes into fields of gold.

We are another crowd, English-speaking,
twentieth-century, listening to our Spanish guide
talk of fifteenth-century tapestries
hung in the Royal Palace.
Our clothes are more diverse, more individuated,
and brightly-colored than the muted swirl
of robes blending on the tapestries.

But caught in mundane details, we often fail
to note the subtleties, especially the faces:
we do not know the way to golden fields;
we have forgot the intricate dance.

But in Canterbury, in Assisi, in Tours,
and now, in this room, I am allowed for a moment
a transcendent vision amid a crowd of faces.
I recognize the hum of bees;
I know the dance that leads to pollen-laden fields;
I stand within a shower of gold.

Pentecost

A pod
blown from
muddy shore
to rock strewn ledge—
fragments—
polyglot:
finally
I locate the right bus.

Last stop.
Climb the mountain,
a thousand meters—there—
follow the path
winding
like the Arno
above rooftiles.

Wall of loafy stones
curled with jasmine;
cinnabar lilies
ring the courtyard:
Santa Margherita.

Perfumes—
tongues of candles.
Soprano.
Vermilion wounds—
black roses brighten
into apple blossoms
blushing for the sun,

petals—wedding veil—
on the grass.

Afterwards—
priest's quarters:
Bianca,
who illuminates manuscripts;
invites us home
for omelets, figs,
pomegranates
and hazelnut gelato.

Ars Moriendi

On the postage stamp of the letter
that arrived today from York,
Europa, blonde, boyish-innocent,
stands, sorrow begun on her youthful brow
and in her downcast eyes.

Dressed in black robe with white shirt-collar,
sword in left hand resting at her side,
before the blood-brown battlements and dark sky,
she stands meditating upon the upper portion
of a skull held in her right hand.

Above this, Queen Elizabeth II's silver profile
stand staring from the upper left corner
through the white expanse before her,
the only sight in her line of vision
the 26p printed at the opposite border.

Glossolalia

Thunder-topped roofs,
chimney-jutted skies,
fog-cold.
Green-dark. Darkness.
Wind. All lines fall.

Then
rising
to a Cam-flooded Common,
we file
like the watercolor-angels
of a Protestant imagination
into the Ridley chapel.

Under jeweled saints-windows,
sixty voices recite the Creed.
We remember the passed,
and the passing—
little boats
no larger than hieroglyphs.

Cambridge Platonism

After long absence,
we sit
in the fading ellipse of November
in Great St. Mary's,
my left arm and leg
parabolic to your right.

A bassoon voice from the shadows
crescendos that God
dwells in dazzling darkness,
the arc of inaccessible light.

Ludgate Hill

1

Last night's coffee grounds
eclipse the sink.
I read the rind of a grapefruit,
a loaf like redundant churches,
molding marmalade.

No holy ground—
which shoes shall I wear?
Outside my shut window
the voice of a child
testing bloated air—

No answer.
　　　No voice.
Morning like cotton.
My feet crowd my chair.

2

Fresh coffee.
Marmalade spread thick
as the yellow crocuses
that awake the sun outside the door.

The bells of St. Paul's—
morningsong, evensong, festival days—
pigeons on the sill
change ring the Sundays of our voices:
all is echo.

Here, where we wear no shoes,
children bristle
through the floors like roses.

Linkings

I wake to the faded straw of the English sun
and see from my window in Linacre House
the frosted lawns and the bleaching ruins
of an old cathedral wall.

A sepia print of my grandmother's last morning
still frames my mind, even here
in the wet October of Canterbury.
In her Colorado hospital bed she lay,
curved like a sickle, discarded
in a September of eighty-three years.

This morning, the cathedral bells
do not summon me.
Nor do the voices of black-robed scholars.
The caving wall becomes my grandmother,
whose loins arched to my mother:
I stand revealed some distance away.

I dress, pack, and walk
past the weather-scrubbed stones in a green
cemetery—the ruins of St. Augustine's Abbey—
to take a patchwork of trains through storms
to the north past York.
The inconvenience, the rains,
do not distract me.

At Whitby I disboard.
In the ruined Abbey I conjure an image
of Caedmon, his red flesh drained,

his white bones bleaching in the sun.
On the still, green grass
stone coffins lie like little boats.

Ulster Sunday

Ushered into darkness
from the curb where I sat
eating stale sandwiches,
past a picture of the sacred heart
lit by an electric candle,
into a sunny sitting room
of three spinster sisters,
I take fresh bread and butter with tea,
while they murmur
against my being on the streets of Derry.
The last bombing was months ago
when their window was shattered;
within two weeks their mother was dead
from the stress of years.

In the graffiti-marked square
two boys point out lists of the dead.
One fingers like a rosary
a plastic bullet
and seems to incant prayers.
In my mind's eye I see headlines of Palestine;
"I'm grateful for plastic," I say.
"It still kills," one boy whispers—
"our brother was hit here"—
pointing to his temple.

From the Protestant sector
that stands like a new Jerusalem,
a city on a hill,
organ music drifts down,

down through fences with barbs
shaped like little stars—
crosses—
knotted scimitars—

Kenmare Runes

Sheep huddle like thoughts
in corners.
The Atlantic spins
in silver coins
over village roofs.

Telephone wires gather
to a low hum,
rails announcing a train.

I take up the receiver.
Lightning on the hills—
Logos in the hand.
Wires resist—
        your voice—
                purple heather—

Afterword

Skies clear.
Wind, roiling leaves remain.
Crucifix-intersections.
Up twelve floors
we sit on Louis XIV chairs.

Distant music.
Pear sherbet
on blue plates.
If our palates
were more refined,
we'd taste our souls.

"Perhaps I can come
to America,"
you say.

My body a bell,
we shake hands,
buss,
in the French way.
I walk to the Métro,
descend.

Three stops later
ascend to Père Lachaise.
ask for a map,
climb
stone-strewn, rambling ways

to Bizet's grave—
then Chopin's.

In leaves
blotted letters
torches
echo hunger.

I turn:
a pear tree shimmers
beneath a round,
blue stone.

Country Dreams

Here where we are warmed
by neat squares
of corn and soybean fields
stitched by loving fingers
into a patchwork
where everything, even belief,
seems cozy,
I could almost believe
that America is home,
blessed above nations;
almost bleach memory
of the Honduran boy
who begged even fishbones
from tourists' plates
to feed a starving sister
wounded by Contra crossfire;
of the lovebites of bruises
that sign the backs of wives and children;
of CIA men sharing the sacrament
of cocaine and armament deals;
of beer cans and wine bottles
stored against famine
behind locked granary doors;
of a rod-wielding actor,
whom many,
wanting a hearthwarmed conscience
and salvific word,
would have followed
to another Red Sea;
of wives who stand

like loaded guns
at their husbands' temples;
of purblind habit,
the unexamined
stitched into pretty hangings.

Home Fires

I must plant. Let fen be home.
Spade turns leaf-mold
from limes, London planes,
Trees of Heaven.

This stirring draws my neighbor's
half-blind, anemic cat.
For a moment I see my cat,
also calico, watching
mountain streams for rainbow trout.

I drop in twelve tulip bulbs,
tuck them with soil.
Leaf-smoke drifts fog-cold
from Sidgwick Avenue.

On winter nights my cat
slept in the curve of my body,
a boat bearing us safely
through the underworld.

In Fitzwilliam's Egyptian collection
three mummified cats
stand like mantel decorations.
On the deaths of favorite horses
cowboys made blankets
from their hides.

Reliquary

I have traveled the world,
viewed finger bones and hairs
wound with wires of gold and silver,
seen the Hapsburgs' guts like soured waltzes
in jars about Vienna.

In an hexagonal cabin in Colorado's Rockies
you undress, removing the locket that contains
fragments of some eastern sage's bones
and place it on the nightstand
beneath a vase of harebells.

Aspens rustle.
Lovely in bone you turn,
taking my hands in yours.
Wind chimes. I kneel.
    Sanctus bells.

Autumn

On the drive down from the Rockies
awhisper with gold-coined aspens
to the sagebrush-mimicked plains,
you brought a bag of Jube Jels,
no larger than a baby's bonnet.
I liked the lemon ones best—
so, like a mother sparrow,
you fed me all the yellow jels.

Then, while we ate cinnamon bread
at my sister's house
you turned—
the wind highlighting sagebrushes
already greying.

Harvest

The song of the meadowlark—Peter, Peter,
Pumpkin Eater—
drifts through the sunlight
like milkweed silk.
From the field of wheat
that bends in the wind
the balloon-breasted bird rises.
The grain is heavy,
nearly ready for bread.

At the window I sit
to bottle-feed my niece.
She wrinkles her nose,
and, with her tongue, pushes
the nipple from her mouth.
Thinking she is about to cry,
I call for my sister,
who comes in song
to cheer the baby,
a petunia in her annatto bonnet.

Naming

One early morning earth's womb opened, and young
Adam,
we are told, gave each new creature a name
proper to its essence:
Adam could see into the heart of things.

Last night you called my name.
Finding me in darkness, you kindled in my breast
a twin to your own firstlight.

Epiphany

Myrtles are evergreens
but delicate, I'd read.
So I removed my potted pair
of miniature crepe myrtles
from the cooling mosaic
of the garden
to the sunny library inside.

By Thanksgiving,
the wheels of fuchsia scallops
had dropped.
The leaves, leathery and emerald,
followed.

I gathered up the pots
on New Year's Day
and, outside, turned one over,
root ball tumbling
to the glacier ground.
Kneeling to examine
a bowed branch,
I glimpsed a streak of malachite.
Placing the fallen myrtle
into its pot, I carried
both plants back inside.

Yesterday, the air was crystalline:
from my library I could almost read
Daniels and Fisher's clock tower.
Glancing at the table,

I noticed the myrtles:
sprouting new leaves--
small and delicate, celery green.

On Nebraska's stubble
you tended your dying father.
When I phoned you--
it was almost St. Valentine's Day--
I couldn't help but say
the myrtles were opening,
leaf by leaf by leaf,
one upon the other.

Felix Culpa

In this Eden
I would stay,
my nostrils dreaming
of the slant-perfume of dawn,
your aubades
granting sight.

But the trees need pruning
to bear fruit next spring—
Italian plums, peaches, red Bartletts,
Jonathans, and Golden Delicious,
hanging like jewels from exotic lobes.

In the orchard I will hear
your song drawing
ecstasy on my left,
my right—spiraling
like incense
to kiss—conceive—me
in this round garden,
the enclosure of your arms.

Cologne

On the steps outside the Dom we stood,
remarking on the pansies still in bloom
in the steely dampness of late November.
You knew pansies as mother-in-laws—
a funny name, I thought, for the innocent
lemon, blue, and burgundy flowers that my mother,
gathering her skirts and kneeling,
taught me to call pansies
when my sentences were yet two-worded.

You stood on one leg, and I, a step lower,
noted your hair wisped like petals
about the collar of your coat.
A citrus scent from the Köln-waser
that we'd dabbed behind your ears drifted my way.
I'd never met someone so happy.

I sit at my window reading the *Fioretti* of St. Francis.
The daffodils outside trumpet their blooms.
I think of St. Clare,
now pomander in an ebony box.
In the drawer of my desk your yellowing letters lie;
since Michaelmas, my aerograms have gone unanswered.

Revision

My shoulders up, as my palms had been
to receive communion at St. John's,
I stop at King Soopers for apples—nice,
crisp, Red Delicious—on sale.
Then I spot you
standing at a checkout counter,
your face toward the man at the register.

I turn and look at the apples—there's another,
firm, without blemish—but glance at you again:
brown eyes and cinnamon-seasoning
of tiny moles about your mouth.
Your hands prayerlike before you,
you stretch—and, smiling,
say something to the checker.

I've found enough apples—
I move quietly.
You do not look my way.
Three registers from you, to your back,
I stand,
and try not to stare. But I find myself
looking at your hair, thinking,

as I survey your back,
that you've lost weight.
You stretch again, perceptible
only to the practiced eye.
I follow the slope of your thighs—

I'm tired of apples, the firm, sweet fruit—

I tell the checkout woman I do not want them.

Love Poem

Betrayal remains the human lot,
bred in us
like spaniels
with a nose for quail.

I am afraid to Judas you—
guts spilled, suicides' trees—

for less than silver
I Judas myself—
                        of your
                        Judasing me—

Holy Communion

Rising
past the fragrance of ankles and thighs,
lingering on chest and neck, to pause
on tiny moles like cinnamon
sprinkled about your mouth

that explored with words, and tongue,
and smile, then to those eyes,
brown as buttered crust on fresh-baked bread;
still I hear your voice, yeasty, low.

Broken from you,
I am set on a shelf apart
from the warmth that gave me taste.
Yet we might priest this separation,
and with open palms and mouths receive ourselves.

As the Crows Fly

Like twelve black tongues
these crows shatter milk-glass sky.
They've come to brag behind the house
in the elm that rises
like a phallus
from winter's belly.

There's no grief here, no grief.
Blackbirds make good pies.
In fairy tales Jacks
kill giants.
Like royalty, Jills
fall down, fetching
with their Jacks
crowned heads.

There's the pail.
This year, no snow.
No wellwater.
Like an envelope
I lick this poem closed.

20/20

Threading from spool to spool
to spool, frost spins
old stories out
over my windows.

Shrunken cherries left by blackbirds
who've read the signs and fled
lie discarded on the lawn.
Like motors, hearts turn—
and turn again—
but refuse, make noise—
absolutely refuse
to start.

Ice covers the city
like a freezer-burned pie.
The fruit trees—no matter their kind—
bear only ice.

Oh *stabat mater*—Jesus—
stoop—
take the cobwebs from the gashes.
Let wounds brighten.
Let us bear fruit
fit for golden bowls.

Acknowledgements

The following poems in this collection were first published as follows:

"Family Portraits," *White Crane Journal*, Winter1998/99.

"Kenmare Runes" (Published as "Prayer,"), *White Crane Journal*, Winter 1998.

"Epiphany," *The Christian Century*, 31 Jan.1996.

"Harvest," *Sisters Today*, November 1995.

"Jacob's Ladder," *First Things,* February 1995.

"Crossroads," *Anglican Theological Review,* Fall 1993.

"Home Fires," "Ludgate Hill," & "Conversion," *Anglican Theological Review*, Summer 1993.

"Ars Moriendi," *Sisters Today,* 6 Nov. 1991.

"Flu," *JAMA*, 13 Feb. 1991.

"Ulster Sunday," *The Christian Century,* 23 Jan. 1991.

"Glossolalia," *Christianity and Literature*, 1990.

"Something to Do with Our Hands," *The Louisville Review*, 1990.

"The Necessity of Symbols," *Christianity and Literature*, 1989.

"A Colorado Spring" & "Augustinian Paradoxes," *the jefferson review*, Fall 1987.

"Cologne," "Incarnation," & "Easter Morning," *St. Luke's Journal of Theology*, 1987.

"Redaction," *Metrosphere*, 1987-88.

"Linkings," *The Louisville Review*, 1985.

"Naming," *Christianity and Literature*, 1984.

"For St. Joan," *St. Luke's Journal of Theology*, 1984.

"On Botticelli's *Madonna of the Magnificat*," *Commonweal*, 16 Dec. 1983.

"Palacio Real, Madrid," *Christianity and Literature*, 1983.

"Iconoclasm," *St. Luke's Journal of Theology*, 1982.
Grave Notions," *The Louisville Review*, 1980.
"The Necessity of Symbols" and "Palacio Real, Madrid,"
in *Imago Dei*, Jill Peláez Baumgaertner, ed., Abilene
Christian Univ. Press, 2012.

I wish to thank a number of people who have helped me
with my poetry in particular. Sena Jeter Naslund and
Alan Naslund have both proved insightful editors and
colleagues, whom I have known since graduate school.
They have helped place my work in several venues.
Fellow poet and editor Jill Peláez Baumgaertner has long
been supportive of my work, seeing that it got published
in several magazines and journals. Former colleague
Colleen Donnelly helped me arrange the order of the
poems in this collection. I also owe a debt of gratitude to
poets Maxine Kumin and Stephen Spender, with whom I
worked for a time in graduate school. My former
colleague Joel Westerholm also gave me valuable
suggestions.

About the Author

One of Thomas Ramey Watson's prominent forebears on his mother's side was Jacques LaRamee. A number of places in the upper Rocky Mountain West bear his name to this day. Laramie, Wyoming is best known. Jacques was a renowned and influential explorer and fur trapper. Because he was just, honest, and treated others, including the often-despised native Americans, well, he was held in high esteem. One winter, the story goes, the native Americans were starving, so they killed one of Ramee's cattle. He told his workers not to say anything—they were hungry. Jacques shared with fellow free trappers his theory that the world was wide and there was room enough for all. He had the courage to live his convictions and followed the beat of his own heart, not what was imposed on him from outside.

One of Ramee's progeny, psychotherapist, life coach, writer, and professor, Thomas Ramey Watson believes that journeying in various realms—of the mind, the physical world, and the soul—is central to enjoying a good life. The insights gleaned from becoming aware of the intersecting planes of existence lead us to fuller and more deeply lived lives.

Thomas Ramey Watson, Ph.D., is an affiliate faculty member of Regis University's College of Professional Studies in Denver, Colorado. He has served as the Episcopal chaplain (lay) for the Auraria Campus in Denver and taught English for the University of Colorado at Denver. He has trained as a psychotherapist and was named a Research Fellow at Berkeley Divinity School at Yale University, a position he did not take, choosing to do postdoctoral work at Cambridge University instead.

He is the author of many scholarly writings, including an acclaimed book on Milton, *Perversions, Originals, and Redemptions in* Paradise Lost. Previews of his forthcoming and published popular writings can be sampled in the pages that follow.

Dr. Watson is available for speaking engagements, teaching assignments, counseling, and coaching. His web address is thomasrameywatson.com, and he can be reached at trw@thomasrameywatson.com.

The first chapter of Thomas Ramey Watson's popular memoir *Baltho, The Dog Who Owned a Man*:

Embracing Mystery

One giant leap—and his front paws landed on my chest. As he stared into my eyes, and I gazed into his, I knew this was the Afghan hound who had been calling me telepathically for weeks. This time, I felt him physically.

I was standing just outside the Denver Afghan Rescue. "You're here," I whispered, sensing his presence. I surveyed the grounds. Dry, tiny-leaved, Chinese elms dabbed a landscape of sagebrush and sand beneath the blazing June sun. "I know it." I walked toward the twelve-foot high, chain-link fence that surrounded the compound, giving it the air of a correctional facility.

As I neared the fence, pebbles crunched underfoot. I opened the gate and walked toward a small, wood-frame house on the west side of the grounds. Dozens of dogs barked, alerting each other and their caretakers to an intruder. I could make out the individual voices of at least fifteen dogs housed there—medium-to-low-range sounds of alarm. Their collective din was excruciating.

A man looked out the window of the house. The door opened. He stepped out into the sunlight and strode my way. He stood at least six-feet-three. He sized me up from head to foot and smiled. I guessed he was Jim, the head of the Rescue—the man I'd talked with last night on the phone. "I'm Jim." He extended his hand. His grip was firm. "Mystery's a super-sized Afghan, weighing seventy-five pounds," he said. "With the build of a linebacker, you ought to be able to handle him. You're what, six-two, maybe two-twenty?"

"Not quite—one ninety-eight."

"Well, you're big enough not to get knocked down." He looked me over again. "Maybe suffer a shoulder dislocation, but only now and then."

I laughed, hoping he was making a joke.

The name the Rescue had given the Afghan hound, Mystery, felt significant. My life was one of paradoxes and mysteries too. If we come into this life with a map, mine was one of roundabouts and detours, with few straight roads anywhere. I was at the Afghan Rescue because I hadn't been able to elude the notion that an Afghan hound was telepathically calling me, begging me, to locate and rescue him. An independent, high-maintenance Afghan wasn't the dog that I'd been planning to adopt. I'd wanted one of those popular breeds—a bouncy, responsive Golden Retriever or a Labrador.

"Mystery's down at the other end," Jim said, walking me out to the pens on the east side of the property. "You said on the phone you're a psychotherapist?" He lifted the heavy padlock on the gate, stuck in a key, and released the lock. He swung open the gate.

I nodded. "I'm just about finished with my training. Until recently, I taught English and was the Episcopal chaplain for the Auraria campus." It was 1992. The glare of the sun on the cement runs and concrete doghouses inside the individual cages made me wish I'd worn sunglasses.

"Good," Jim began. "You're complicated. You should be able to understand Mystery, if anyone can." He laughed.

"I've spent my whole life trying to understand mysteries," I said. "It seems something is always trying to outfox us, threatening our best-laid plans. I'd like to see what's ahead and avert the danger before it manifests."

Jim laughed. He closed the gate behind us. "This reminds me—you've got to be careful about latches of every kind. Mystery is smart, often too smart. He can open just about any gate. A strong padlock—kept locked—is the only guarantee of confining him."

We passed into an alley that must have stretched at least a hundred yards ahead. Individual kennels formed by six-foot high chain-link fencing lined the way. Each kennel was maybe eight-feet wide and twelve-feet deep and contained a square dog house made of cement at the back. Some kennels held one or two Afghans. Some were empty.

As we walked, I spotted a frail, small-boned, white Afghan. *There's a Snow Queen in hiding*, I thought. Her body was shaking. She stared up at me with brown, soulful eyes. She looked pitiful, so needy. The rescuer in me wanted to respond.

"The dog for you is this way," Jim said, urging me on. He was several yards ahead of me by then. The place was a labyrinth. I wondered where the Minotaur was.

We took a few more steps, and a huge, dark beast bounded from a distant side-run into our path. His long, brindle hair, as I'd learned to call it during my earlier years with an Afghan, flew from his sides like magnificent wings.

"Mystery's out!" Jim shouted—as the Afghan bounded past him toward me, barking excitedly.

I had only time to mutter, "Mystery's everywhere," before he skidded, reared up, and, with his front paws, landed on my chest. Remarkably, he was so graceful that he didn't knock me over. I did, however, feel the impact of his muscle-driven mass.

Still barking—then whimpering and yapping alternate-ly, as if he'd found his long-lost partner and friend—he nipped at my nose, my earlobes, my chin.

"Hey," I said, "I know you're ecstatic, but take it easy with the biting. It hurts."

In the bright sunshine, his thick, dark coat showed a glossy mix of walnut browns and mahoganies, highlighted by Brazilian teaks and blonds. The hair revealed a distinct red cast.

A big white star with a long tail ran the length of his chest. His dark whiskers, also showing red highlights, formed a full and bushy beard, the greatest I'd ever sighted on an Afghan. His eyebrows must have been an inch long, and his intelligent eyes, like rich cherry wood, complemented his coat.

He began to pet me with first one paw and then the other. His toes moved upon me, massaging my skin. I noticed the huge, webbed feet that his breed had evolved. Their toes became webbed so they could gain better traction in desert sands, helping them grasp unstable terrain. Their upward-curved tails could be tracked above desert scrub.

"I think you've got yourself a dog." Jim laughed. "As soon as you leave here, you'd better search for the largest carrier crate you can find. Put Mystery in it when you aren't around. Even though we think he's five or six, he needs security. That'll keep your house safe when you're gone."

I recalled Jim's telling me on the phone that the woman who'd first adopted him said he'd ripped up her bedding and chewed a hole the size of a watermelon in the middle of her mattress. "He peed and pooped everywhere," Jim had said. "So she returned him to us."

"On the phone, you told me you knew something about Afghans, didn't you?" Jim asked. We'd already been through this, but Jim wanted assurance.

I nodded.

"They're sight hounds," he said, repeating what he'd told me earlier. "They see something and take off."

"I got my previous Afghan as soon as my divorce went through," I said. "I've long been drawn to Afghans. I don't know why. I had my Afghan, Oriana, for years."

Mystery wrapped his legs tightly around my chest, as if to hug me tight, never to let go. He fussed, whimpered happily, and yapped away. The distraction was welcome. I didn't want to dwell on the past, certainly not my bad marriage and divorce.

I looked into Mystery's eyes. "Oh dog, I know you're the one." Tears welled in my eyes. For weeks, he'd been tweaking the telepathic connection, finding my frequency. "I need you—rescue me!" he'd broadcast. "You are mine. I am yours."

I lowered my head, so his cheek pressed against mine. "I am yours, and you are mine—for as long as we're given." By then, I could hardly speak. I hugged him tightly, gathered my wits, and opened my mouth, but the words remained only in thought. *Hello, willful, curious—beautiful—swift-as-the-wind, Afghan. Hello, Mystery, my friend.*

A preview of Thomas Ramey Watson's forthcoming novel:

Reading the Signs: A Paranormal Love Story

Synopsis

Ted Jones, university campus chaplain and English Professor in Denver, doesn't need more problems. His life has been full of them. Yet, at the beseeching of the spirit of an old woman, he becomes involved with Sharon, the woman's grown granddaughter. Damaged though she is, Sharon responds. Although Sharon and Ted's trials are multiple, their love forms the crux of the novel. Such love reaches beyond time and space as we normally conceive them, to involve intersecting planes of existence that touch both past and future.

Chapter 1: Vision

The bells of St. Elizabeth's, loud and dissonant, blended for a moment before becoming strident again. They brought back memories of studies in Italy. There, such bells rang out from the landscape and tumbled across the hills into cerulean seas. Here in Denver, the sounds reverberated across campus to snow-covered peaks and reminded me of melodies rising from chaos.

I walked toward the church. The sun shone brightly. A blizzard had blanketed the city the week before, but this morning felt warm. The snow had almost vanished, even in shaded areas. Overnight, the grass had turned from straw to dewy green. Crocuses were bursting into small purple, white, and yellow stars. Like Persephone, spring had returned from Hades, decked in flowery gowns of green. The cycle of life had begun again.

From the sidewalk in front of St. Elizabeth's, I heard a voice. It was coming from the roof. My eyes traveled up the gray granite blocks to a white statue of Mary, a bouquet of roses carved in her hand. I moved my eyes to the stained-glass window behind the statue. The voice came from there.

I stood still and concentrated. I shifted my consciousness slightly to the side. Mystical experiences were not new to me. I'd experienced a number of these phenomena over my thirty-three years. As a professor of English, I specialized in the Great Philosophical and Theological Tradition of the Western World. I'd read the mystics and saints. I was also the Episcopal chaplain for the colleges sharing the Auraria campus.

The apparition of an old woman floating in mid-air appeared near the rose window, a smaller version of those adorning the great cathedrals of Europe. Like a mist moving across the building, her body looked translucent, as fragile as rice paper. Her white hair was pinned at the back, with loose strands falling about the deep wrinkles of her face. Again, she called my name and began to speak in a language that sounded like Russian. She gestured for me to come closer.

www.ingramcontent.com/pod-product-compliance
Lightning Source LLC
Chambersburg PA
CBHW020950030426

42339CB00004B/32